# World Soccer Stars ⚽ Estrellas del fútbol mundial

# Lionel Messi

## José María Obregón

English translation: Megan Benson

**PowerKiDS** press

**Editorial Buenas Letras™**
New York

Published in 2009 by The Rosen Publishing Group, Inc.
29 East 21st Street, New York, NY 10010

First Edition

Editor: Nicole Pristash
Book Design: Nelson Sa
Layout Design: Julio Gil

Photo Credits: Cover (left), pp. 7, 13 (main), 21 (main) © AFP/Getty Images; cover (right), pp. 5, 9, 11, 13 (background), 17, 21 (background) © Getty Images; pp. 15, 19 © Bongarts/Getty Images.

Library of Congress Cataloging-in-Publication Data

Obregón, José María, 1963–
  Lionel Messi / José María Obregón. — 1st ed.
     p. cm. — (World soccer stars = Estrellas del fútbol mundial)
  English and Spanish.
  Includes bibliographical references and index.
  ISBN 978-1-4358-2729-5 (library binding)
  1. Messi, Lionel, 1987– —Juvenile literature. 2. Soccer players—Argentina—Biography—Juvenile literature. 3. Short people—Argentina—Biography—Juvenile literature. I. Title.
  GV942.7.M398O37 2009
  796.334092—dc22

  [B]
                                      2008027170

Manufactured in the United States of America

# Contents

# Contenido

Lionel Messi is one of the best soccer players in the world. Messi was born on June 24, 1987, in Rosario, Argentina.

Lionel Messi es uno de los mejores futbolistas del mundo. Messi nació el 24 de junio de 1987, en Rosario, Argentina.

Messi has been playing soccer since he was very young. When he was eight years old, he played for the youth team of Newell's Old Boys, one of the best teams in Argentina.

Desde pequeño, Messi demostró ser muy bueno para el fútbol. A los ocho años ya jugaba en las fuerzas inferiores de Newell's Old Boys, uno de los mejores equipos de Argentina.

Messi was born with an illness that makes him shorter than other people. When he was a kid, he needed a costly **treatment** for his illness, but his family did not have the money to pay for it.

Messi es muy bajito porque nació con una enfermedad. De niño, Messi necesitaba de un **tratamiento** muy caro para su enfermedad, pero su familia no tenía el dinero para pagarlo.

FC Barcelona, a Spanish team, offered to pay for Messi's treatment because he was such a good player. Messi then became a member of the team when he was 13 years old.

Como Lionel era muy buen jugador, el FC Barcelona, un equipo de España, ofreció pagar por el tratamiento. A los 13 años, Lionel se unió al FC Barcelona.

In May 2005, Messi became the youngest player to score a **goal** with FC Barcelona. Messi was 17 years old!

En mayo de 2005, Messi se convirtió en el jugador más joven en **anotar** un gol con el FC Barcelona. ¡Messi tenía 17 años!

That same year, Messi helped the Argentinean soccer team win the U-20 **World Cup**. This is the World Cup for players under the age of 20. Messi was named the best player in the cup.

Ese año, Messi ayudó a la selección de Argentina a ganar el Mundial sub-20. Esta es la **Copa del Mundo** para jugadores menores de 20 años. Messi fue el mejor jugador de la copa.

Messi plays striker position. He moves very fast, and it is hard to take the ball away from him. Messi's teammates call him the flea. A flea is a small bug known for how fast it moves and jumps.

Messi juega como delantero. Messi se mueve muy rápido y es muy difícil quitarle el balón. Sus compañeros le llaman la Pulga. Una pulga es un insecto pequeño que se mueve y salta muy rápido.

Messi helped Barcelona win the Spanish **tournament** in 2005 and 2006 and the European Champions League in 2006.

Messi ayudó al Barcelona a ganar el **campeonato** de España en 2005 y 2006 y la Liga de Campeones de Europa en 2006.

Lionel Messi works very hard to help kids. He is a part of the ASPIRE Academy of Sports Excellence, in Qatar. This school helps children who are good at sports.

Lionel Messi trabaja para ayudar a los niños. Messi forma parte de la Academia de Excelencia Deportiva ASPIRE, de Qatar. Esta escuela ayuda a niños que son buenos para el deporte.

# Glossary / Glosario

**goal (gohl)** When someone puts the ball in the net to score a point.

**tournament (tor**-nuh-ment) A group of games to decide the best team.

**treatment (treet**-ment) Drugs and other attention given by doctors.

**World Cup (wur**-uld **kup)** A soccer tournament that takes place every four years with teams from around the world.

---

**anotar** Conseguir uno o varios goles.

**campeonato (el)** Grupo de partidos que deciden cuál es el equipo campeón.

**Copa del Mundo (la)** Competición de fútbol, cada 4 años, en la que juegan los mejores equipos del mundo.

**tratamiento (el)** Cuando se le da atención médica a una persona.

# Resources / Recursos

## Books in English/Libros en inglés

Shea, Therese. *Soccer Stars*. Danbury, CT: Children's Press, 2007.

## Bilingual Books/Libros bilingües

Contró, Arturo. *Cristiano Ronaldo*. New York: Rosen Publishing/Buenas Letras, 2008.

## Web Sites

Due to the changing nature of Internet links, Rosen Publishing has developed an online list of Web sites related to the subject of this book. This site is updated regularly. Please use this link to access the list:

www.buenasletraslinks.com/ss/messi/

# Index

# Índice